One Woman's Gold Rush

Snapshots from Mollie Brackett's Lost Photo Album

1898-1899

Historical Research and Text by
Cynthia Brackett Driscoll

Oak Woods Media

Library of Congress Cataloging-in-Publication Data

Driscoll, Cynthia Brackett, 1935-
    One woman's gold rush : snapshots from Mollie Brackett's lost photo album, 1898-1899 / historical
research and text by Cynthia Brackett Driscoll.
        p.   cm.
    ISBN 0-88196-007-1 (pbk.)
    1. Klondike River Valley (Yukon)--Gold discoveries--Pictorial works. 2. Klondike River Valley (Yukon)--Gold
discoveries. 3. Frontier and pioneer life--Yukon Territory--Klondike River Valley. 4. Frontier and pioneer life--Alaska--
Skagway. 5. Women pioneers--Yukon Territory--Klondike River Valley. 6. Women pioneers--Alaska--Skagway. 7.
Skagway (Alaska)--Social life and customs. 8. Brackett, Mollie. I. Brackett, Mollie. II. Title.
F1095.K5D75 1996
971.9'1--dc20   96-12942
                                                                                                    CIP

Printed in the United States of America
with soy-based ink on recycled paper

Published by Oak Woods Media
PO Box 19127
Kalamazoo MI 49019
(616) 375-5621

ISBN 0-88196-007-1

Dedicated to the memory of Pattilyn Drewery.
If she had been alive in 1898,
she surely would have been here, too!

Acknowledgments

If my father John Chapin Brackett and my uncle Russell Dibble Brackett had not been foresighted enough to recognize that the life of their grandfather George Augustus Brackett as a Minnesota and Alaska pioneer might interest historians, my research would not have been possible. Because of them, many of George A. Brackett's papers are tucked safely in the archives of the Minnesota Historical Society. I would like to thank the personnel there for their courtesy, knowledge and helpfulness.

My cousins Dianne and David Brackett have been generous in sharing their papers, my cousin Judd Brackett and my first-cousin-once-removed Mary Brackett Ballard likewise. Mary, 88 years old in 1996, gracious and keen, remembers her Aunt Mollie Brackett fondly, so it was especially delightful to talk with her.

Writers need research librarians. For their skill and help I am grateful to Nancy Noble, special collections librarian at the Portsmouth, New Hampshire Public Library; Jane Porter, keeper, Portsmouth Athenaeum; Michael McGinnis, librarian, Itasca Community College, Grand Rapids, Minnesota; Signe Carsted, research specialist and Janet Crawford, chief librarian, Grand Rapids Public Library.

Many thanks to Candy Rossbach and Peter Reasoner, Itasca Community College's knowledgeable computer specialists.

Thank you David Curl, then a complete stranger, for calling me in September 1995 with an idea for a book.

And especially, thank you my friend and partner Todd Driscoll for your support these 34 creative years.

— *Cynthia Brackett Driscoll, January 1996*

Contents

Foreword

"We feel as if this woman is alive today and we're sneaking a look into her diary."

I am sitting one morning in my cubicle office at the Anchorage Public Television station when in walks my friend Pat Worcester. He lays on my desk an old-fashioned, laced-up scrapbook. He says, "Take a look at these pictures and tell me what you think."

The curious little prints are bright blue, they are very old, and there are a lot of them.

On the front cover of the torn black album is embossed the word *PHOTOGRAPHS*. Inside, in fading ink, but inscribed with a bold feminine hand, is written: *Mary Montgomery Brackett, Skagway, Alaska. Begins in 1898.*

Both of us forget the day's deadlines as we leaf carefully through these crumbling, yellowed pages with the tiny, oddly trimmed blue images pasted onto them.

We feel as if this woman is alive today and we're sneaking a look into her diary. The pictures are personal glimpses of her friends, her family, and her life on a strange frontier. She has penned notes and dates beneath most of her snapshots. We step back nearly a hundred years to the time when Mary Montgomery Brackett was a young bride, thrilling to the adventure of a lifetime. We go back with her to the Klondike Gold Rush and meet the bold, bright Brackett clan whose business enterprises would leave their mark in the history of northwest transportation and mining.

Pat tells me more about the amazing history of the album. He says it was found in the trunk of a repossessed car by a southern California auto salesman named Robert Wilson. Robert gave the album to his brother, Richard, who passed it on to a friend's daughter, Pattilyn Drewery, who lived in Alaska. After Pattilyn's untimely death in 1991, her family, knowing that Pattilyn treasured the album because

Pattilyn Drewery, like Mollie Brackett, was an Alaskan pioneer. A communications project director in Anchorage, Pattilyn was an enthusiastic proponent of Alaska. Mollie Brackett's photo album would have been among the prized possessions of both women, and Pattilyn had intended to make Mollie's pictures available to museums so more people could experience Alaska's history.

of its historical value, gave it to Pattilyn's close friend, Pat Worcester. Pat knows that KAKM is looking for pictures of the Gold Rush for a Centennial video; and so, here sits Pat in my office and the two of us are totally enthralled.

That incredible tale covers only a couple of years in the life of this old album. We're wondering where it rested since Mary Brackett last laid aside these mementos of her youth. What fortune or providence put the old loose leaf book into that California car trunk and guided it safely through a chain of steady hands to the stewardship of Pattilyn and Patrick?

Later, Diane Brenner at the Anchorage Museum of Art and History explains to me that the strange blue 19th Century images are cyanotypes and that they retain their color and clarity because they have been kept in their original album, in the dark. Enlarged reproductions of the photographs now are available for research and reference in the permanent collections of both the Klondike Gold Rush National Historical Park in Skagway, and the Skagway Trail of '98 Museum, thanks to the efforts of Clay Alderson, Karl Gurcke, Judy Munns and Dave Curl.

Cynthia Brackett Driscoll has been inspired by her great-aunt's photographs to write this book as a tribute to the historical legacy left to us by Mary Montgomery Brackett.

— *Tom Morgan, Producer/Director, KAKM Alaska Public Television*

Significant Snapshots

"The amateur, capturing candid and sometimes intimate moments in the everyday lives of his or her family members, preserves memories ..."

People sometimes belittle snapshots as "poor" photographs; but simple, amateur photographs, like personal letters and diaries, give us precious glimpses into the past. Thanks to a turn-of-the-century "Kodak" craze, images exist to enrich our understanding of those fascinating times. Searching for meaningful pictures is like panning for gold — historians sift through a mound of sand and gravel to find an occasional nugget. But some of those nuggets fill the pages of this book.

Amateur snapshots tend to be made from a different viewpoint than professional photographs. Two pictures may be taken of the same scene, but they will be from different angles and with different purposes. The amateur, capturing candid and sometimes intimate moments in the everyday lives of his or her family members and friends, preserves memories; always in the forefront of the professional's thoughts is making a living. Competent professional photographers such as E. A. Hegg, H. C. Barley, Asahel Curtis and Winter & Pond were in business along the Gold Rush trails. Their livelihood depended on commercial commissions and print sales.

Amateur photos, snapped with small hand held cameras, are less sharp than professional images, more grainy, sometimes blurred. But their fresh viewpoint makes these photos more revealing of attitudes, customs and costumes of the time.

Most professional photographs of the late 19th century were carefully composed on the ground glass of a large wooden view camera mounted on a sturdy tripod. The glass plate negatives usually were 8"x10" in size. But these

THE HAWKEYE JUNIOR CAMERA.

No. 6507. Many people appreciate a camera which can be used for either roll films or glass plates, as it enables them to use either, depending upon the circumstances. If only a few pictures are to be made and developed, glass plates can be used to the best advantage, but if going off on a trip where a large number of pictures are to be taken, the films to the average individual are considered most desirable. The Hawkeye Junior camera takes a picture 3½x3½ inches. The

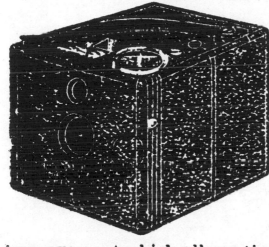

outside dimensions of the case are 4¼x4½x6 inches and weighs but 20 ounces. The case is well made, is covered throughout with best grain leather and is supplied with neat carrying handle. The lens is the single achromatic offset focus, very rapid and capable of doing good work indoors as well as in the open air. The shutter is supplied with a late improvement which allows time exposures to be made without danger of jarring the camera, which is the difficulty experienced when undertaking to make such exposures with the majority of small cameras. The speed can be regulated for snap shots, which will properly time the negative even in a weak light, and is provided with an improved indicator for counting the number of exposures which never fails. The automatic tally always shows at a glance the number of pictures which have been taken. A brilliant square view finder centers the view accurately upon the surface of the film.

Price of the Hawkeye Junior covered with black grain leather, without roll of film, or plate holder. Each..$7.20
Double Dry Plate Holder for dry plates. Each.. .90
Sunlight Film for twelve exposures. Per roll... .55

This camera may be the kind used by Mollie Brackett. As advertised in the 1897 Sears, Roebuck catalog, its 3 1/2-inch square format and provision for time exposures are consistent with the pictures she took. Mollie's good friend Mrs. Tuckerman is holding a camera like this in the photo on page 53.

Mollie was interested in the children and animals around Skagway. In this unintentional "self-portrait," her shadow fills the foreground.

BRSGY067

"... sometimes amateur snap-shots are the only images available to historians."

needle-sharp images generally were formally posed and seldom show the spontaneity reflected by humble snap-shots made with smaller cameras.

According to Karl Gurcke, cultural resources specialist at Klondike Gold Rush National Historical Park, sometimes amateur snapshots are the only images available to historians. For example, Mary Montgomery Brackett's pictures of the Fantail Trail between Log Cabin and Atlin, British Columbia are the only such views known to us. Perhaps there are other pictures of this heavily traveled winter route and of the early Atlin mining operations in a Canadian archive or in a private collection, but these tiny blue cyanotypes in Mollie's album certainly appear to be unique. Among Mollie's photos are a picture of the present Golden North Hotel when the large frame building stood on its original site at 3rd Ave. and State St. In 1898 it was Sylvester's Store. Ten years later the building was jacked up on logs and towed to 3rd and Broadway where a third story was added and the dome was painted gold. Also a view of Ben Moore's House from the mountainside verifies details of fencing and outbuildings not visible in other photos.

The sharpness and clarity of the snapshots from the pages of Mollie Brackett's Gold Rush photo album do not begin to match the quality of professional photographs of the day, yet they offer us priceless windows into the past. They breath life into the bodies and show us the forgotten faces of people who, without these pictures, would forever remain unfamiliar names on crumbling newsprint.

— *David H. Curl*

White Pass Pioneers

"... Captain William Moore ... claimed that because the White Pass was less steep than the ... Chilkoot ... strings of pack animals could travel all the way to Lake Bennett."

For most stampeders in 1897 and 1898, the race for gold meant choosing between two tortuous trails. Both routes notched through the 6,000 ft. mountain range that shields the Canadian interior from the coast of southeast Alaska, and each way had its enthusiastic boosters. Once across the mountain barrier, the gold fields lay some 450 miles still farther north across a chain of lakes and down the raging Yukon River to Dawson City. Each "argonaut," as the gold-seekers were known, was required to haul a ton of food and supplies from tidewater over the pass, clear Canadian customs, then perilously paddle and float to the Klondike.

The undeveloped White Pass Trail was six miles longer than the Chilkoot, which was an established Tlingit Indian trade route. But Captain William Moore, who had first explored the White Pass, claimed that because the White Pass was less steep than the boulder-strewn Chilkoot summit approach, strings of pack animals could travel all the way to Lake Bennett.

Moore, a talkative man, was also an irrepressible optimist. Furthermore, he had strong business reasons to encourage tens of thousands of travelers to disembark at his Skagway wharf instead of at the nearby rival town of Dyea, head of the Chilkoot Trail.

When the 65-year-old Moore and his Indian companion Skookum Jim hiked over the White Pass route ten years earlier, the ground proved solid enough except for some boggy spots beyond the summit. But when the stampeders began to arrive, horse traffic soon churned thawing soil into knee deep mud, slowing the pace and causing packers to turn back in impatience and disgust. The mud and steep,

"... when most men his age were planning retirement, Brackett mobilized his resources [and set out for Skagway ...]"

narrow slopes turned the so-called "trail" into a slaughter hole for 3,000 animals, whose decaying corpses washed for months down the rocky valley of the Skagway River. Moore's vaunted White Pass Trail had become the dreaded "Dead Horse" Trail.

Opportunity attracts entrepreneurs. Quick money could be made by transporting people and goods over those mountains, so other eyes were fixed upon the White Pass. A railroad was needed. A lucrative freight and passenger monopoly awaited the first syndicate powerful enough to cut through Canadian and American bureaucracy for permission, clever and persistent enough to blast track bed from sheer granite in wintertime, and rich enough to finance the venture.

One who shared this vision was George Augustus Brackett, former mayor of Minneapolis. Experienced in building railways that opened the American West, Brackett arrived in Skagway intent on profiting from the provisioning of prospectors, but soon realized that a permanent Yukon-to-the-sea transportation link would be both imperative and profitable. He also saw that the difficult White Pass was the only practical route. In the autumn of 1897, when most men his age were planning retirement, Brackett mobilized his resources and, with help from four of his seven sons, hoped to rebuild his financial situation lost in the depression following the Panic of 1893.

Brackett's enterprise was undercapitalized from the start. Instead of building a railroad, he struggled to raise enough cash to blast, grade and pave, with logs and gravel, a rough but level toll road over the most impassable parts of the Dead Horse Trail, bridging rivers and ravines and

13

skirting around the worst bottlenecks. Brackett's railroad dream was finally crushed when the British-financed White Pass and Yukon Corporation bought him out. The narrow-gauge railway, rushed to completion at the summit by February 1899 and connecting with river steamboats at Whitehorse by July 1900, still operates antique cars out of Skagway as a seasonal tourist attraction.

The White Pass & Yukon Route railroad remained the Yukon's only year-round land connection until completion of the Alaska Highway during World War II. But a shorter highway was needed that followed the route taken by gold-seekers from Skagway. So in 1978 construction began on scenic Klondike Highway 2, which was officially dedicated in 1981 as "The Trail of '98." Captain William Moore's vision is honored by a cantelever bridge bearing his name that spans Moore Creek gorge 11 miles north of Skagway. But the names of the other great White Pass pioneers — Michael Heney, who built the railroad, and George Augustus Brackett, who *wanted* to build it — remain obscured by the shadows of history.

— *David H. Curl*

From Woman's Standpoint

This and the following reprint of contemporary newspaper articles set the stage for the arrival on the Alaska frontier of Mary Montgomery (Mollie) Brackett. The original spelling, punctuation and grammar have been retained.

"Delicate women have no right attempting the trip ...Those who love luxury, comfort and ease would better remain at home."

THE SKAGUAY NEWS   DECEMBER 31, 1897

From Woman's Standpoint
By Annie Hall Strong

Hints to Women
What Should be Taken and What Should be Left Behind
Other Points of Value and Interest

Women have made up their minds to go to the Klondike, so there is no use trying to discourage them, for

"When a woman will, she will,
And you may depend on it."

When our fathers, husbands and brothers decided to go, so did we, and our wills are strong and courage unfailing.

We will not be drawbacks nor hindrances, and they won't have to return on our account.

We go to encourage, to assist, and help provide for their bodily comforts.

There are a few things, however, a woman should carefully consider before starting out on this really perilous journey.

First of all, delicate women have no right attempting the trip. It means utter collapse. Those who love luxury, comfort and ease would better remain at home.

It takes strong, healthy, courageous women to stand the terrible hardships that must necessarily be endured.

15

The following suggestions may be of some value to those who are contemplating making the trip next spring.

My experience thus far has shown me the necessity of women being properly clothed and equipped for the trip to the interior, and I can speak with some assurance, having been especially observant along this line. First and most important of all, by far, to be considered is the selection of proper footwear.

It is not necessary to have shoes two or three sizes larger than one's actual last, simply because you are going on a trip to the Klondike. Get a shoe that fits, and if the sole is not very heavy have an extra one added. The list that follows is the very least a woman should start with:

1 pair house slippers.
1 pair knitted slippers.
1 pair heavy soled walking shoes.
1 pair arctics.
1 pair felt boots.
1 pair German socks.
1 pair heavy gum boots.
1 pair ice creepers.
3 pair heavy all-wool stockings.
3 pair summer stockings.

Moccasins can be purchased here of the Indians. The tall bicycle shoe with extra sole would make an excellent walking shoe. A pair of rubbers fitted to these might come in handy during the rainy season.

In the way of wearing apparel a woman can comfortably get along with:

1 good dress.

"A ready sewed tick will be nice to have, for it can be filled with dried moss and makes a good pioneer mattress."

1 suit heavy mackinaw, waist and bloomers.
1 summer suit, waist and bloomers.
3 short skirts of heavy duck or denim, to
    wear over bloomers.
3 suits winter underwear.
3 suits summer underwear.
1 chamois undervest.
1 long sack nightdress, made of eiderdown or
    flannel.
1 cotton nightdress.
2 pair Arctic mittens.
1 pair heavy wool gloves.
1 cap.
1 Arctic hood.
1 hat with brim broad enough to hold the
    mosquito netting away from the face.
1 summer dress.
3 aprons.
2 wrappers.
2 shirt waists.
Snow glasses.
Some sort of gloves for summer wear, to
    protect the hands from mosquitoes.

BEDDING

1 piece canvas, 5x14 feet.
1 rubber blanket.
3 or better 4 pair all-wool blankets.
1 feather pillow.

A ready sewed tick will be nice to have, for it can be
filled with dried moss and makes a good pioneer mattress.

17

"... all the old Yukoners take in a goodly supply [of butter]. The miners say pure grease makes a pleasant drink."

An old miner would no doubt laugh me to scorn for suggesting a little satchel or handbag, but the comfort derived from one hundred and one little iotas a woman can deftly stow away in it will doubly repay the bother of carrying it.

In the matter of outfitting in the commissary department, one can follow, as a rule, almost to the letter, the lists that have been published over and over again by leading outfitters.

From actual experience I find evaporated eggs a failure, and every one who took saccharin as a substitute for sugar are loud in their condemnation of it. Take plenty of sugar. One craves it, and 200 pounds per outfit is not too much.

The lists fail to mention butter, on account of its being looked upon as a luxury, but all the old Yukoners take in a goodly supply. Some carry the tub butter, while others prefer the 2-pound tins. The miners say pure grease makes a pleasant drink. If so, butter will certainly not be amiss.

Corn meal, sugar, tea and coffee should be packed in tins.

Take plenty of tea.

Fifty pounds of rolled oats is the usual amount mentioned on the lists, but 100 pounds is far better.

Baking powder and candles are apt to be the first articles to disappear. A few extra pounds would come in very handy if one were where these articles could not be purchased.

Dried blackberries or raspberries make a delicious dish mixed with dried apples, and are a change.

"Take both white and pink beans, for one grows tired of them, and a variety may lessen the degree of weariness."

Take both white and pink beans, for one grows tired of them, and a variety may lessen the degree of weariness.

Lemonade tablets are preferable to lime juice and citric acid, being easier to carry, having no weight or bulk.

The evaporated goods are a grand success. The onions, soup vegetables, and minced potatoes being especially palatable.

A good-sized mess box with a hinge cover and lock containing enough food for the trip will be found a great convenience and avoids the necessity and extra work of opening sacks and boxes at every camp, besides being especially handy for the cook.

The following is a list of what the box may contain.

Flour.
Bacon.
Beans.
Rice.
Sugar.
Cornmeal.
Extract of beef.
Baking powder.
Yeast cake.
Salt.
Pepper.
Pilot bread.
Prunes.
Dried fruits.
Canned roast beef and tongue.
Chocolate.
Condensed cream.

Most of us know how unpleasant it is to live in a trunk, but when an Alaskan outfit is packed and hammered down in a canvas bag it is a whole day's work to find anything.

I have succeeded in making a little improvement in packing some parts of the outfit. With three canvas bags, one used exclusively for bedding, one for wearing apparel and a third for foot wear of all kinds, lots of unnecessary unpacking and repacking can be avoided.

Several people who have used the sleeping bags have been sadly disappointed in them. A piece of heavy canvas 5x14 feet will take the place of the heavy, inconvenient, ready made sleeping bag. Fold half the strip of canvas on the ground, place your bedding on it and draw the other half over you. You are thus protected from the dampness and wind and have something doubly useful, for if you are caught out in a blizzard without a tent you can stretch your canvas over a pole and make a tent at a moment's notice.

— *Annie Hill Strong*

Impressions of Skaguay

THE SKAGWAY NEWS   DECEMBER 31, 1897

Before and After Taking. What I Expected to Find and What I did Find in the New Metropolis

By Annie Hall Strong

"Cut throats and mobs of evil-doers were said to form the population, and it was alleged that they lay in wait for the arrival of 'tenderfeet.'"

Women pioneers hold an honored place in the history and development of the west and great northwest; and when the history of the development of Alaska, and the great interior region, known as the Yukon country, shall have been written, it will be found that women have played no inconsequential part therein.

There are two sides to the life of a woman pioneer. One represents hardships and privations — hope deferred, which maketh the heart sick, trials and disappointments. The other presents fuel for the spirit of adventure, and its attendant excitement, leading one on and on in the hope — in this case — of golden reward, and the fondest fruitions of one's most cherished dreams.

When the most contagious of all fevers, known as "gold fever," began to rage I was among the first to contract "acute Klondicitis" and immediately started northward to the land of "plenty of gold."

The awful tales of suffering and privation counted for naught as long as shining nuggets were to be the reward. All went well until we reached Juneau and here my heart almost failed me for, judging from the terrible tales told by returning and disheartened gold seekers, I was to fall among riff-raff of the whole country at a place called Skaguay, which was the initial point of the congested White pass. Cut throats and mobs of evil-doers were said to form the population, and it was alleged that they lay in wait for

"... I found a surging crowd of people ... but ... no one attempted to rob or mob. Everyone was kind, and those that were already settled assisted in every possible way ..."

the arrival of "tenderfeet." Was it any wonder I hoped the time would be long ere we reached the awful place?

However on the morning of the 26th of August we steamed around a point into a bay and right before us lay the really beautifully situated little tent city.

It looked peaceful enough from the deck of the steamship Queen, but the faces of the future Eldorado kings looked anxious and for once I remained behind while the gentlemen of our party went ashore to find a camping place, thinking I would just as soon postpone my entrance into this modern Sodom until it became compulsory.

Towards evening, with fear and dread, I actually ventured ashore. To my surprise I found a surging crowd of people busy as bees rushing hither and thither — but everything was orderly and quiet. No one attempted to rob or mob. Everyone was kind, and those that were already settled assisted in every possible way to smooth over the rough places and brighten camp life for the argonauts.

There appeared to be a general feeling of bonhomie between these friends of a day. Kindness was the watchword; there was no evidence of violence or crime — nothing but kindness.

Such were the people of this much maligned town the day I landed, and there has been no change, and, in saying this, I think I voice the experience of every woman found within the confines of Skaguay.

But the little tented town is a thing of the past, and in its stead has sprung a bustling town of 3,000 souls, and we old settlers that have grown up with the place during the past three months, are proud of our town. Skaguay is the

"... Skaguay will be the principal gateway to the interior."

baby city of the world in age, but come look at her and be amazed!

We have a church and a school house. We boast electric lights, a telephone system and other adjuncts of modern civilization, and when our tramway and wagon road shall have been completed, Skaguay will be the principal gateway to the interior. Brave, staunch and upright citizens built Skaguay, not riff-raff, hence our prosperity.

A. H. S.

Looking up Broadway - Skagway

BRSGY002

Skagway - Looking West.

BRSGY003

One Woman's Gold Rush

Gold talk hovered in the air, and a poke filled with yellow dust and soft gold nuggets could buy a shot of whiskey or a two story, clapboard hotel. By early February 1898 when Mary Emmeline Montgomery (Mollie) Brackett stepped onto Moore's Wharf with her camera, Skagway, Alaska had become the northernmost vestige of America's lawless western frontier.

Newcomers were advised to steer clear of Jefferson Randolph "Soapy" Smith's gang of bunco artists and "sure thing" men. These silk-tongued hoodlums took advantage of the greed and naivety of unwary arriving "cheechakos," while their associates pinched the pokes of careless "sourdoughs" returning rich from the Klondike.

Skagway was booming. Ragtime piano tinkled through the night at saloons with names like The Red Onion, The Hot Scotch, and The Mascot. Gunfire was heard often enough to frighten visitors, and carpenters' hammers rang and saws buzzed throughout the long arctic twilight. Residents who slept at all awoke to count five new wood frame buildings completed each day, with more than 700 permanent structures rising above the tents in the four months since August 1897. Every week at least two steamships were scheduled to arrive in Skagway from Seattle.

Down the gangplank of each overloaded ship streamed hundreds of black garbed men toting crates and bags full of food and supplies, eager to begin a more formidable journey than any of them knew. Neither the men nor the few hardy women among them fully understood the challenge they faced — struggling by foot or by sledge over either the White Pass or the Chilkoot Pass, and down over 400 miles

BRSGY030

Moore's Wharf: Arrival of
"City of Seattle:"

25

Mary's wedding portrait, 1896

of difficult Yukon River waterway to their fortunes.

The muddy little tent city into which Annie Hall Strong had disembarked in late summer had, by the new year of 1898, become a boisterous Gold Rush boom town. While Strong wrote in the newspapers of her experiences, another adventurous young woman, Mollie Brackett, would leave a powerful pictorial record of those historic times.

Before she landed in Skagway, Mollie may have read both of Annie Strong's articles in the December 31, 1897 issue of *The Skaguay News,* which had been published just one month earlier. Mollie's 61-year-old father-in-law George A. Brackett had sailed to Skagway to regain his fortune in September 1897, sending his 21-year-old son James before him to sell a load of cattle. Planning to sell food and supplies to the miners, George Brackett also hoped to provide some pioneering experiences for his seven sons. He communicated often with his big family back in Minneapolis enclosing issues of *The Skaguay News,* and his letters and enclosures whetted his sons' and Mollie's appetites for adventure. Although she had grown up leading a life of culture and gentility in a large eastern city, Mollie was eager to share the future with her new husband, George's third son Thomas Thayer Brackett.

On October 27, 1897 George wrote from Seattle to his son Chapin (Chape):

You ask too many questions about this country that I find it difficult to take them up in detail, and may neglect answering some owing to limited time. Will say, however, that the work I have in hand will not admit of my making any promises to you and Tom, but as it

Thomas Thayer Brackett

develops think it possible that I may be able to make some arrangement that will be advantageous to you both. I have taken hold with Judge Acklen and others to start this road over the Skaguay Pass. You understand, of course, there is much detail to be entered into before I can do as I would like, as the law in Alaska will not admit of the construction of a toll road without act of Congress, which does not meet until December. ... I shall, however, go to Skaguay and commence work and push as rapidly as possible, taking chances of the necessary legislation. I have just closed a contract for a 250' span railroad bridge to cross the main canyon, which is in fact the key to the situation on the Skaguay river; having the right to collect toll over this bridge gives us possession of the one pass over which a railroad or wagon road can be built. We already have men at work at that point.

Frank soon followed Jim and their father to Alaska, leaving brothers Al, Dave, Chape and Tom itching to follow. Youngest son, Karl, would visit later. Even Mollie was early caught up in the lure of the family's Gold Rush adventure. On October 23, 1897 Tom wrote to his father that Mary was considering withdrawing her money from her brother Horace's music business in Portsmouth, New Hampshire to invest in the wagon road her father-in-law was building over the route of the White Pass trail from Skagway to Lake Bennett.

In his return letter on October 28, 1897, George A. Brackett at first responded cautiously, but soon was overcome by his own enthusiasm:

I think now that I have opportunity to invest it to

George Augustus Brackett and his seven sons at their summer home on Orono Point, Lake Minnetonka, Minnesota. Left to right (youngest to oldest): Karl, Frank, Jim, Chape, Tom, Dave, Al, and the patriarch.

George Augustus Brackett

bring her a much larger return than she is now receiving, but I want it distinctly understood that I invest it where I invest my own, having full faith that it will return to me a good income for what I put in, but she must take the same chances and the same responsibility that I am taking; I am perfectly willing to put my money into the enterprise and if she permits hers to be used in the same way, she must take the same chances I do; but I shall be more than cautious in what I do with it. If she sees fit to send it here in draft care of C. E. Peabody, I would only use it when I am thoroughly satisfied that it is right. Opportunities are offered here every day, and I think I never have seen so much enthusiasm and so active a community as I find here, and everyone looking to the Clondyke [sic]; I say every one, I mean the majority; I am not a Clondyke man; I am only watching opportunities, and the little gold that I dig shall be in enterprises forwarding the interests of those who are going to the Clondyke. See my letter to Chape in relation to my wagon road enterprise and to Dave and Al relating to other matters. I find life to [sic] short to go into details with seven boys, I am therefore covering business with one, social relations with another, etc.

Mollie Montgomery had married into a large and lusty family of seven "boys," as their father still called them even though most were now young men, and one girl, Susie. George Brackett's wife and his children's beloved mother Annie Hoit had died in 1890, when Karl, the youngest, was just 8. Susie suddenly had "entire charge of [the] two homes and a houseful of six brothers." Only the eldest, Al, had by

29

then married and moved out. For two years, until 1892, when she married Harry Whitney Dowling, a Washington , D. C. native, their sister played mother to her noisy, talented, energetic, attractive batch of brothers.

Now, after the country's financial recession of 1893, father George, in "reduced circumstances" and still with a number of dependents, was risking a "great enterprise." With what he had determined was "ample capital," he had started building a wagon road for gold-hungry miners to haul their gear from the wharves of Skagway, Alaska over the White Pass to Lake Bennett, British Columbia, a distance of approximately 40 miles. Brackett was convinced that the White Pass was the best route to the Yukon River, Dawson and gold. By charging toll, he expected to take advantage of one of the many opportunities of the gold rush. In early 1898 he found a job for Tom.

So on January 7, 1898, Tom had *"Rec'd of Geo. A. Brackett the sum of $275 (Two hundred & seventy five dollars) to be returned on [his] arrival in Skaguay."* Mollie and Tom, married only one year and four months and with the optimism of forward-looking youths, were on their way. On February 4, *The Skaguay News* reported *"Mr. and Mrs. T. T. Brackett are recent additions to Skaguay. Mr. Brackett is the son of George A. Brackett. Mrs. Brackett is an accomplished musician."*

Born into a prosperous musical family in 1870 — her father owned Montgomery's Music in Portsmouth, New Hampshire — Mollie grew up singing and playing the piano. In her twenties she became a voice teacher, "brilliant singer" and member of the "quartette of the Middle Street

Mary Montgomery Brackett

30

Three Little Chinese "Y. Y. 73"

Baptist church." Since he was fond of music, Tom may have met Mollie at a musical engagement in Boston when he attended the Boston School of Technology. After her marriage and move to Minneapolis, she was the "well-known soprano soloist at Westminster Presbyterian Church." But Mollie may have tired of drawing room society and church engagements.

Mollie welcomed the move to Alaska. She was ready to record through her lens her own views of the Alaska/British Columbia/Yukon gold rush, scenes that E. A. Hegg and H. C. Barley, professional photographers at work in Skagway in these early years, may have thought too commonplace. Her photographs are, for the modern historian, another form of gold. She began with Skagway.

While Tom helped his father build the wagon road and packed supplies over the pass for the firm of Hinkle & O'Brien, Mary organized the Brackett household, aided her sister-in-law Ida, Al's wife, with her four children, and snapped her shutter at the Skagway scene: streets of the booming city; "Father Brackett's first Home in Skaguay from Sept. '97 to February 1898," the Bay View Hotel; Brackett's Trading Post, her brother-in-law Jim Brackett's second and larger Trading Post selling meat, food and complete outfits for traveling miners; her new friend Mrs. Tuckerman hanging out her wash with a terrier on a rope; "Sylvester's Store and apartment house," an elaborate two story building with many display windows; inside views of her father-in-law's house: the "Music corner in the living room at the Mansion House;" "Writing desk corner southeast. Father [asleep] on couch;" "Siwash" Indian squaws

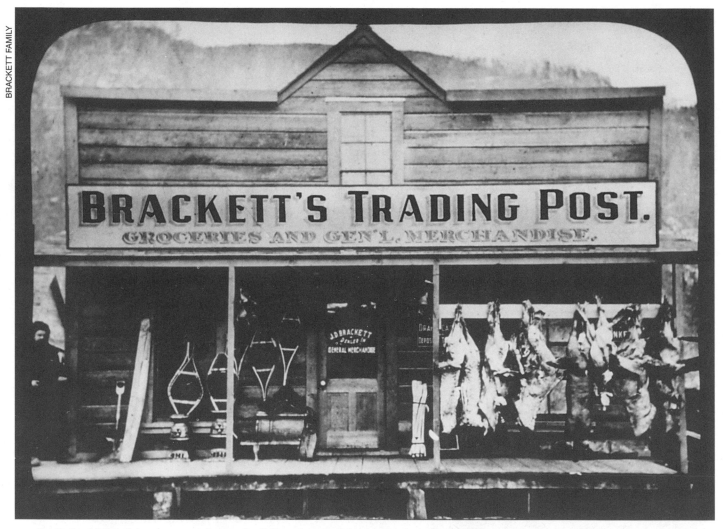

Built in 1897, this one-story frame building housed the business operated by Jim Brackett. After the Bracketts moved into larger quarters it became the Boss Bakery. Moved to its present site on Broadway north of 5th, the building was restored in 1985-1986 by the National Park Service and became a clothing and gift shop.

Just Home in Skagway from Sept. 97
February - 1898.

BRSGY018

George Brackett lived here at the Bay View Hotel on Fourth Avenue during his first months in Skagway. The Golden North Hotel, which moved in 1908 into the domed building it now occupies, is next door (right).

This two-story Brackett building, erected at Third and Main in Skagway early in 1898, was referred to by the family as "The Mansion House." The comfortable living quarters photographed by Mollie probably were upstairs where the fancy curtains can be seen. The sign appears to have been moved from the former store building shown on page 32.

BRSGY086

February. 1898.

34

Nellie. "G. A. B" Miedreath Mrs Jane
Fannie

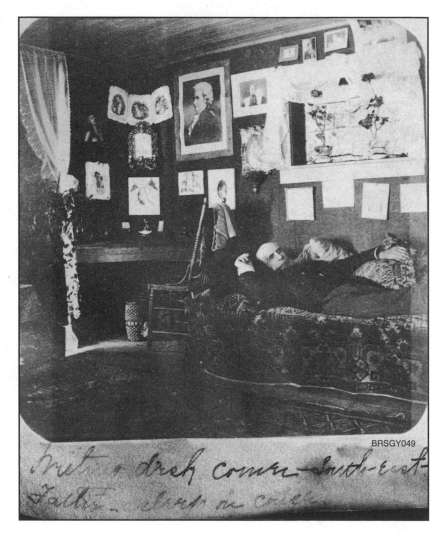

BRSGY052

*"Library Corner of Dining-room.
Chilcat Indian
blanket hanging
on the wall."*

BRSGY056

The "dining-room-end"

BRSGY049

*Writing desk corner South-east
Father asleep on couch*

36

Cosy-North-West-corner.

Lavatory-corner.

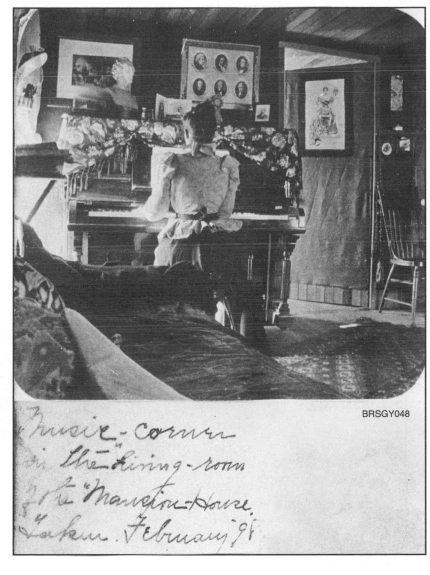

Music-corner
in the "Living-room"
of the "Mansion-House"
Taken February '98

"Sylvester's Store" and xxxxxx House. Corner of Third Avenue and State St.

BRSGY021

38

BRSGY009

A huge halibut caught near Skagway. 1898.

BRSGY032

The Wrecked "Mercury March 1897"

*Skagway is a seaport — The Taiya
Inlet is a deep water fjord — so
Mollie's attention was drawn to
everything from shipwrecks to fishing.*

"Aint m plain":
Indian Matters

BRSGY084

40

RESTAURANT

BRSGY047

"Nice=boy" and a set g' "things"
February - 1898.

"Nice boy" Tom is second from right, wearing boutonniere.

Typical Chilkat Indian Children.

BRHNS004

These youngsters were photographed during an excursion by boat to nearby Haines Mission. The Skagway valley had never been home to a large native population, but some Tlingit traders and packers involved themselves in the commerce of the growing town. The slang term "Siwash," meaning provincial or commonplace, was sometimes applied in those days by whites referring to Indians.

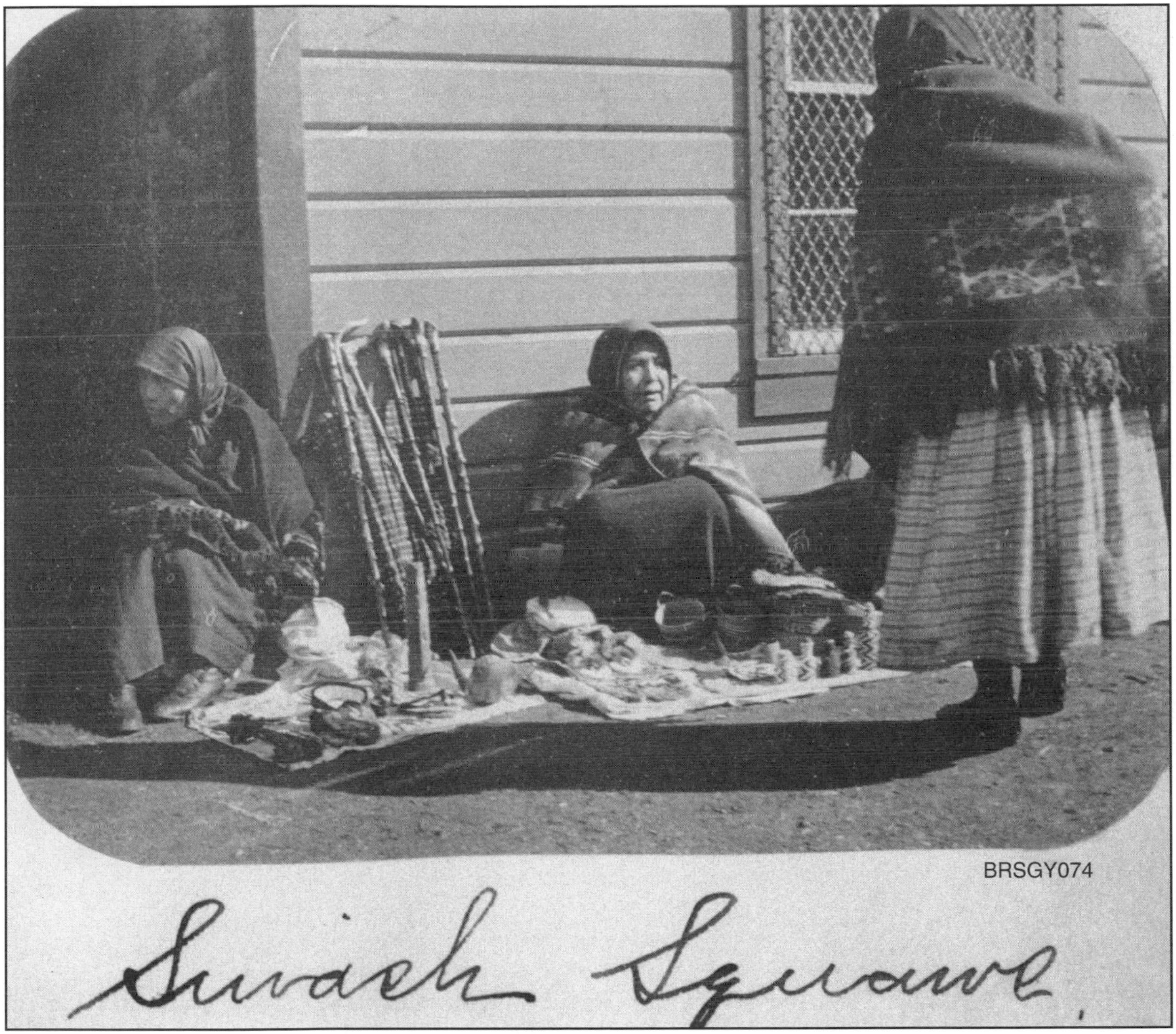
BRSGY074
Siwash Squaws.

WAGON ROAD THROUGH THE CUTOFF 3½ MILES FROM THE SUMMIT OF WHITE PASS.
COPYRIGHT 1898 E. A. HEGG SKAGWAY

194.

By winter, thanks to back-breaking labor the White Pass trail was still difficult, but passable. This E. A. Hegg view looking up the valley toward the summit shows how Brackett's crews had improved the way.

At right, the first wagon road bridge nears completion. The Skagway River valley was a major obstacle to traffic, so Brackett's 250' corduroy log bridge was a top priority. Notice that this image is a double exposure — probably unintentional art created by the photographer forgetting to advance the film.

44

BRWHP118

Bridge & Miss Morrill.

George Brackett (center, kneeling, wearing billed cap) confers with financiers and engineers. This photo shows clearly how bridges were built along the wagon road — logs were laid crosswise over log stringers supported by log and stone cribbing. The available timber would have been mainly spruce. Only fragments of the stonework and rock ballast remain today due to rotting of the wood and blasting by railroad crews working on the slopes above.

Opening of the key bridge over the Skagway River valley. From this angle, the couple in the carriage certainly resemble Tom and Mollie. In other photos she is seen wearing an identical jaunty feathered hat.

TAKE NOTICE! BEGINNING March

TOLL WILL BE COLLECTED

ON ... D FROM NEAR THE 1ST BRIDGE THROUGH WHITE PASS.

G. A. BRACKETT.

BRWHP115.

"Old. Bob." one of the few Surviving
the original trail horses.

"General Brackett's Claim" *(caption handwritten below photo, BRWHP101)*

"Working goats on the trail March-1898" *(caption handwritten below photo, BRWHP107)*

selling handmade pipes, baskets and moccasins; and steamships at Moore's Wharf.

She handed a friend the camera to snap her on a wharf with an Indian man and captioned it, "Ain't we Plain. Indian Matters." She captured her husband Tom enjoying the mountain scenery and later wrote beneath the photo, "Nice-boy and a cart of 'Mugs' February 1898." "Three Little Chums of T. T. B." reveals two young boys and a girl perching on a Yukon sled, their English setter dog by their side.

In mid-February 1898, Mollie's curiosity got the best of her; the trail beckoned. Father-in-law George — the "little general" she sometimes called him — had completed enough of the wagon road, including a few bridges, to begin charging tolls. As Brackett's men began nailing up toll gates, the miners and packers, accustomed to towing their Yukon sleds over the much improved former "dead horse" trail without paying fees, rebelled. By ganging together they easily overpowered the gatekeepers, often tossing them over the embankments after their broken gates. On February 15th *The Skaguay News* headlines read, "Toll Gate Fight [A]gain Resumed." Probably discussed over dinner nightly, this news was too interesting to disregard. Mollie took to the outback to see the excitement for herself. She saw much more, recording it all through the lens of her square, black box camera.

In one snapshot "'Old Bob,' one of the few survivors of the original trail horses," stands in front of a sign stating, "TAKE NOTICE! BEGINNING MARCH 1 TOLL WILL BE COLLECTED ON THE TOLL ROAD FROM NEAR THE 1st BRIDGE THROUGH WHITE PASS, G. A. Brackett." In an-

BRWHP167

Frank Brackett digging out his tent at the Summit Feb. 99

A Winter Home

BHWHP149

other, "Working goats on the trail, March 1898," Mollie shot harnessed goats, shaggy with thick winter pelts, pulling a sled up the trail. She is interested in everything. "'General' Brackett on 'Charger'" catches George Brackett sitting high in his saddle. In the background are stacks of barrels, lumber and a large, round ax-sharpening stone at one of the White Pass trail worker camps, while son Al stands smiling at the head of the horse. Everyday life on the trail, construction as well as controversy, is well documented by Mollie Brackett, the amateur camera buff. But through her eyes, we can see, too, another aspect of the Brackett family's life in the Alaska of the 1890s.

"A Winter Home" shows a small tent with a glass window and wooden door, smoke blowing out a stack, pile of fire wood ready and a dog waiting patiently. Tom had become a packer, and it is possible he and Mollie spent some nights in this trailside abode. (Winter temperatures, moderate at sea level in Skagway, often plummeted to -20° and below on the trail with high winds forcing wind chill down much further.) In February 1899 Mollie snapped her brother-in-law "Frank Brackett digging out his tent at the Summit" showing a similar small tent and Frank, who was just 17 when he was called to Alaska by his father, standing on five feet of snow trying to uncover his tent. Mollie was adventuring farther than she had ever dreamed. Alaska was *very* far from her comfortable family home on the corner of Merrimac and Miller in Portsmouth, New Hampshire.

But Mollie was in her element. Adventure twinkles in her eyes in many of the photographs. She shows her playfulness and good humor when she captions a photo of

Naughty Mary + Old Gust.

Two little Maids from Skaguay.

BRSGY098

herself and a man who probably was one of her father-in-law's employees "Naughty Mary and old Gust." Proper hat atop her head, gloves on against the chill of mountain air, she stands near one of the Brackett wagon road corduroy bridges, the white of snow on the mountains behind her, old Gust gazing at her profile. Attired as a lady should be in long wool skirt and leg-of-mutton sleeved wool jacket with large military-style buttons, she looks with level gaze at the camera. In "Two little Maids from Skaguay" Mollie poses provocatively, smiling and swishing her skirts at the photographer (her husband Tom?) while her friend Mrs. Tuckerman, with bland expression and neutral body language, sits, cradling her own Hawkeye box camera, on a length of water pipe which is waiting to be buried under the unpaved street.

A snapshot of a hatted man at work near Log Cabin, with wash hanging on the line, is entitled, "I just *love* to saw wood. Now watch me." Another caption of a scene overlooking a lake, of men, tent, loaded horse, cache of many piled boxes states, "Puzzle, Find Tommie." Mollie is on the trail with her husband and a group of packers. Packing and camping in the mountains over a steep and often snowy pass is hard work, and in 1898 it entailed risk and danger. A woman among men had to be not only courageous, but hardy and good humored as well. Weather delays, horse and equipment breakdowns, risk of robbery or animal attack were always present. The newest American frontier, especially away from the more civilized Skagway, posed unknown threats and possible severe hardship including losing one's way. Packing over the White

BRWHP130

"I just love to saw wood. Now watch me."

Puzzle, Find Tommie.

BRWHP142

Crusty, loquacious Captain William Moore was an original Skagway pioneer and the first to realize the potential of the White Pass route.

BRSGY028

BRSGY039

"Oscar" after the horse kicked him

Cousin Oscar raised horses to be sold in Skagway. The Montana ranch land for this enterprise probably was owned by George A. Brackett.

"City of Seattle"

BRSGY031

BRSGY079

Dead horses. Skaguay
River Bottom. April 1899.

BRSGY046

Off for Reids Falls June '95

Pass was not for weaklings.

Skagway newspapermen and women, local retailers, the steamship lines and George Brackett were promoting Skagway and the wagon road at every opportunity. Delays in its construction caused back-ups on the trail and bad publicity for Skagway businesses.

From the first shovelful of dirt and the first dynamite blast of boulders, George Brackett's great enterprise had been financially taxed. Judge J. H. Acklen, a former Tennessee congressman, and the local business people who had formed the Skaguay and Yukon Transportation & Improvement Company came forth with little of the promised cash. Workers, many funding their trips to Dawson by blasting rock and building cribbing on the wagon road, demanded cash, and Brackett, left in the lurch by the company's financial backers, scrambled to acquire enough to meet his payroll. His frequent trips to Seattle, Boston and Washington, D C. seeking investors appeared to some as if he were dodging his responsibilities. This time he was slapped with a law suit.

On June 3, 1898 *The Skaguay News,* always interested in the wagon road, reported:

The Bracket [sic] Wagon Road has been placed in the hands of a receiver, and Dennis M. Brogan, one of the proprietors of the Occidental Hotel, has been appointed by Judge Johnson to act in such capacity.... It is to be hoped that matters will be speedily adjusted, so that all parties interested will receive the money due them, the receiver discharged and the work of construction pushed forward rapidly.

"... Less than twenty days after our first intimation that [Skaguay would have a railroad] hundreds of men were actually engaged in its construction."

But by June 17th, headlines in *The Skaguay News* stated, "Brackett Again in Charge." "*...A strong aid to Brackett, in having the order appointing a receiver revoked, was that a petition signed by the majority of Brackett's creditors, and by 35 laborers now employed by him on the road, was presented to the court in corroboration of the plea made by the attorneys....*" Another in a long string of crises was at least temporarily over. Brackett returned to Skagway in early July having *"succeeded in procuring all the funds necessary to pay off the men ... and all the other accounts past due."* The Brackett family in Skagway was becoming used to the controversy that accompanies pioneering ventures.

The Skaguay News proclaimed Skagway to be "A MARVELOUS CITY" on July 1. 1898, predicting that the little city "[was] entering the threshold of an era of prosperity unparalleled in the annals of Alaskan history." Prosperity was to come *"in the shape of the Skaguay and Lake Bennett railroad — the first and only line ... that anyone had ever, in the wildest flights of imagination, dreamed that Skaguay would have. ... Less than twenty days after our first intimation that we were to have such an improvement, ... hundreds of men were actually engaged in its construction."*

George Brackett did not want Klondike-bound packers shipping their loads by railroad — at least one that was not of *his* making — before he had earned back his expenses and made a profit for his investors. The Canadian railroad builders feared cut-rate competition from Brackett's rival wagon road, yet they needed the road to transport supplies

"First prize for the best female waltzer ... imported perfume case. Second prize ... pair of ladies shoes."

to construction sites not yet accessible by rail. From a weak bargaining position George had been negotiating all spring with the railroaders. Finally he agreed to accept substantially less than the asking price on his "great enterprise" while defiantly persuading the Canadians to agree to allow him to continue collecting tolls on the Brackett wagon road until the railroad was completed. This compromise would mean a premature end to their freight business, so some major decisions would have to be made by George and his tribe of hard working sons.

Meanwhile Skagway was reveling in self-glorification. *The Skaguay News* stated, *"Here we can glorify and jollify with the full assurance that in no spot in the entire Union does the bright sun of prosperity beam more effulgently and with greater radiance than here in Skaguay, the metropolis of the northwest, the marvel of the last decade of the nineteenth century."*

The Fourth of July and its traditional celebration may have come at just the right time for the Brackett family, who needed a bit of levity. *The Daily Alaskan* highlighted the *"First prize for the best female waltzer, No. 2 extra fine imported perfume case, Second prize, for lady, pair of ladies shoes."* By summer '98 there were enough women in Skagway to arrange parties and events encouraging community togetherness and patriotic spirit.

Mollie participated in the day-long festivities, photographing the street parade. Wagons decorated as floats bumped along uneven dirt streets, patriotic colors flying. A child dressed to the teeth in a white suit and white top hat sat in a sled pulled by a dog. Men fill the scenes; hardly a

BRSGY076

A portion of the Fourth
of July. Street parade.

"Fourth of July parade.
"Bill Lazarus" one of the "long-time miners"

BRSGY036

65

BRSGY027

Excitement at City Hall during the arrest & trial of the "Soapy Smith gang"

"Since women were so scarce in this frontier boom town, they were much appreciated and attended to at social occasions."

woman is visible. And we may be sure Mollie enjoyed the evening's activities. Since women were so scarce in this frontier boom town, they were much appreciated and attended to at social occasions.

Then on July 7th, Mollie Brackett photographed the crowd outside City Hall during one of the most exciting events of her tenure in Skagway. All day long, throngs of men milled about while the little city's movers and shakers tried to decide what to do. *The Skaguay News* EXTRA tells the story:

...The cause which led up to the trouble ... had its origin in the morning shortly before 10 o'clock when J. D. Stewart, a young man just out from Dawson, was robbed of a sack containing from 12 to 15 pounds of gold. There are conflicting stories as to how the robbery was committed, the accepted version being that Stewart desired to sell his gold, and that one Bowers, a well known member of [Soapy] Smith's gang, represented to Stewart that he was here for the purpose of buying gold for some big assaying company below. The unsuspecting stranger accompanied Bowers to a point to the rear of Smith's place on Holly [A]ve., ... where, it is alleged, two of Bowers' pals were in waiting, when the three men overpowered Stewart, wrested the sack of gold, containing $2670, from his hands, and disappeared ... leaving the returned Klondiker as poor as when he started for the land of gold and hardships nearly a year before.

As soon as the news of the bold and daring broad daylight robbery became circulated about the city, there was fire of indignation. People were inexpressibly sur-

The notorious "Soapy Smith's gambling saloon.

BRSGY007

"... the indignant townsmen formed a committee to 'devise ways and means of ridding the city of the lawless element.'"

prised and shocked that such a flagrant outrage should have been committed in the city. Business men quietly discussed the situation, and, feeling assured that it was Smith's men who did the job, many of the best and most influential of our city went quietly to the leader and informed him that the gold must be returned, and that he and his gang must shake the dust of Skaguay off their feet. During the earlier part of the excitement, Smith partially promised several men, including the writer, that, in case there was no "roar" made in the papers, the gold would be returned by 4 o'clock last evening, and that his influence would be used to prevent his men from in any way interfering with returning Klondikers in the future.

The gold hadn't been returned by four o'clock as promised, and Smith was drinking heavily. At eight o'clock the indignant townsmen formed a committee to "devise ways and means of ridding the city of the lawless element." They stationed themselves at the end of Juneau dock to confer, guarded by another committee of four when

Jeff Smith appeared carrying a Winchester ... He walked straight up to [Frank] Reid and with an oath, asked what he was doing there, at the same time striking him with the barrel of the gun. Reid grabbed the gun in his left hand as it decended [sic], pushing it down towards the ground, and drawing his revolver with his right hand at the same time. When the point of the rifle was close against Reid's right groin, Smith pulled the trigger. The ball passed clear through and came out through the lower part of the right hip. At about the same time Reid fired two or three shots in rapid succession, one of which

"Be my careful."

BRSGY033

"Did you mention anything about getting a "bite""

BRSGY089

pierced Smith's heart ... Both men fell at about the same time, "Soapy" Smith stone dead and City Engineer Reid dangerously, perhaps mortally, wounded.

The citizens of the little city of Skagway patroled the streets all that night. The next day, business was suspended until as many as could be found of Soapy's gang were rounded up. Even "the entire trail from Skaguay to Bennett [was] closely watched." Mollie's photo entitled, "Excitement at City Hall during the arrest & trial of the Soapy Smith gang," shows horses and men milling about in front of City Hall. It was a very tense time.

Summer excursions in July 1898 softened the often harsh, always interesting frontier life of the Brackett young people and their friends. On July 15th, "Geo. A. Brackett left on the Tartar [a steamship] on a hurried business [trip] to the Sound cities." Tom and Mollie relaxed, taking a day jaunt up the wagon road with their friends the Tuckermans and the Cheneys. Discovering a downed tree over the shallow Skagway River, they decided to cross it. One shot shows Mollie and Mrs. Tuckerman balancing gingerly as they step across. Each wears an ankle length skirt and a jaunty hat with a six-inch upright decoration. Mollie holds up her skirt and steps carefully in the middle of the round trunk. Mrs. Tuckerman leans forward, separating branches as she tries to step through them. They are, as the caption states, being "very careful." In another delightful, if fuzzy, shot, Mollie and Tom fish from the same tree, long poles out over the water, Mollie's toes curling as if to keep her from falling in, Tom squatting, both smiling with full enjoyment of their precarious situation. The caption, "Did you

The Summit Lake... [handwritten caption]
BRWHP177

Summit Lake. [handwritten caption]
BRWHP178

mention anything about getting a bite?" catches their mutual enjoyment. This is one of the reasons Mollie married Tom, one of her reasons to risk an Alaskan adventure — pure fun.

One of the most telling shots shows Mollie, Tom and Mrs. Cheney probably on the Skagway wagon road. Entitled "Throw-out-your-chest," it demonstrates the close relationship between Tom and Mollie. Bracing her hand on Tom's shoulder, Mollie steadies her position on a roadside log while he gazes at her smiling. At the split second the shutter clicks, neither seems aware of Mrs. Cheney or the photographer.

On a longer Summit Lake excursion, the three couples slept overnight in a tent "Six in a bed," ate a picnic "Dinner at the Summit" and posed "On the Summit" in their summer garb, the men in sporty caps, the women in high boots and leg-of-mutton sleeved jackets. Mollie's high-crowned straw hat is a stand-out. The series of eight snapshots of this trip certainly exhibit the women's sense of adventure in the Alaskan outback. "Mrs. Cheney climbing over the rocks on a trip down from the Summit. July '98" reveals just what conditions the women were willing to risk for a few days of recreation.

In August, Mollie took advantage of an offer by the new railroad of a free excursion. As yet there were no enclosed passenger cars, so railroad personnel placed rows of chairs on flat cars and started the train up Broadway from the wharves. In her photo "Starting up Broadway" women and men are crowded together on the cars on what would seem today rather precarious seating, especially

BRSGY092

"Throw·out·Your·Chest."

Ascending Porcupine Hill · March '98

Summit Camp

BRWHP172

"Grandpa Turk" making his toilet
at Summit Camp. Canadian custom house
upper left hand corner.

BRWHP175

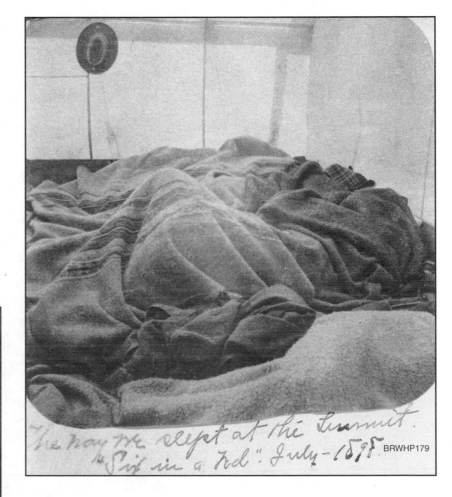

The way we slept at the Summit.
"Six in a bed". July - 1898.

BRWHP179

Mrs. Tuckerman. "I" Mrs. Cheney Mr. C. Lomme
Mr. Tuckerman. +
On the Summit.

BRWHP174

Dinner at the Summit

BRWHP173

75

Mrs. Cherry climbing over the rocks on trip down from Summit. July '95

BRWHP181

76

THE IDAHO.

ADING COMPANY

BEER

BRSGY038

Starting up Broadway.

BRSGY037

An Excursion up the rail-road August 1898.

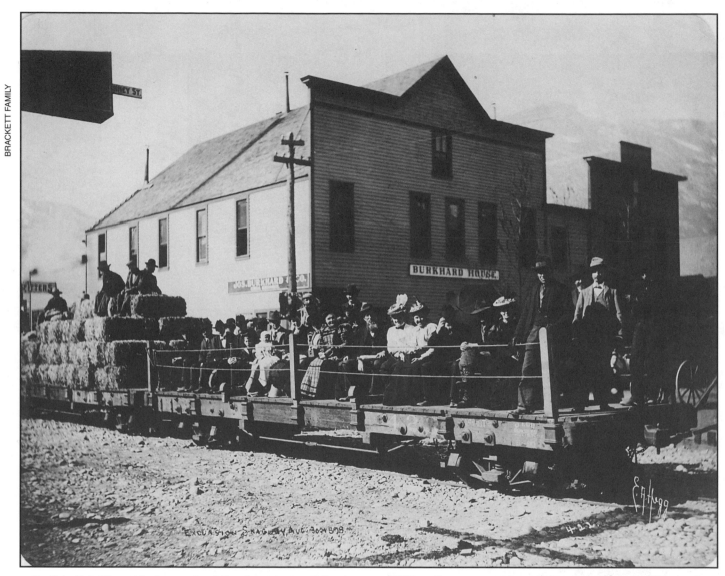

In this E. A. Hegg photograph of the departure of the August 1898 railway excursion, George Brackett, Mollie, and Mrs. Tuckerman are seated on the flat car just below and to the left of the Burkhard House sign.

White Pass - City. R. R. grades at top of picture

BRWHP140

White Pass City was a major resting point on the original White Pass trail to the summit. Bypassed by the railroad, all that remains here today along the river bank is an archeological site.

Camp-Mine - Wagon Road
A pack-train.

BRWHP150

80

BRATL009

"Heetops just where we feel hungry."

BRWHP162

A Crush at the Summit.

The steepest hill on the Road from Skaguay to Atlin

BRATL010

The "Log Cabin, headquarters of the
N. W. Mounted Police

BRWHP170

Log Cabin, looking East from Custom House.

BRWHP165

BRATL007

The "Olive May" ready to leave Bennett.

BRATL030

"Ships Ahoy!—. "We were obliged
to "lay to;" on account of a
"prairie schooner."

Taku "City" November
1898

BRATL008

At Taku, the men were hunting their freight

"O yes, I am a "Jack at all trades."

Wm E. Haseltine

Brackett & Hazeltine's store as it
looked the morning we arrived in Atlin.
Our sled

Whipsawing by the
Northern Lights

BRATL002

Atlin Pioneers.

BRATL006

since the train clacked over high crib bridges and around cliff hugging bends. Until the railroad track was completed and enclosed parlor cars arrived, each with its own wood-burning stove, breathtaking excursions on open flat cars were a major Skagway tourist attraction.

In Skagway on August 9, 1898 *The Daily Alaskan* published a story of the new gold strike on Pine Creek in Atlin, British Columbia, just 85 miles east-northeast of Skagway. "The mining fever has spread right to the wharf, and agent Twitchell has caught it. This afternoon he was studying how to affix wings on to his bicycle, so that he might go in to the new diggings from Log Cabin."

By August 20th, *The Skaguay News's* EXTRA edition bore a gigantic headline that read "RICH AS THE KLONDIKE IS PINE CREEK NEAR ATLIN." Within sixteen days of the strike, "a town site had been laid out at the lake and named Atlin City." Lots had *"been sold at prices ranging from $150 to $350, and several stores and restaurants [had] been started. Meals [were] $1.00 each, ham was selling for $1.50 per lb. bacon $1.00 and gold pans $5.00."* Already on August 11th 50 camps were busy, and on August 20th, the fever had reached record pitch. Atlin and gold had become a new focus for the Brackett family, and Mollie was there.

By late fall the adventurous Mollie Brackett was recording the new trail to Atlin by rugged wagon road and open water. Mollie's "Taku 'City' November 1898," the tent city and way station between Taku Arm of Tagish Lake and Atlin Lake, reveals caches of goods under tarpaulins, a sled, a lapstrake dory overturned, white tents and one cabin.

"I am the monarch of all I survey"

BRATL011

Interior of our Atlin Cabin

BRATL014

Snow covers the ground, and smoke rises from stacks. Two men saw a board from a tree trunk in "Whipsawing by the Northern Lights." "Atlin Pioneers" stand in front of their roughsawn log cabin. "A dangerous place on the Atlin trail" is evident as two men lean their weight against a loaded one horse sledge, preventing it from overturning.

On the unimproved Atlin trail novice prospectors lost their way while experienced miners, knowing what to wear and to transport, usually arrived in good shape. Tom felt confident, because he and Mollie became part of an early winter party of three horses pulling five sledges. "We stop just where we feel hungry" is a snowy scene, horses with feed bags and people resting and eating while crossing a lake, sparse black spruce covering the white land rising from lakeside. Mollie snapped "The steepest hill on the road from Skaguay to Atlin" where at the top of a hill, a man with a sled is contemplating the slide down.

In "Brackett & Hazeltine's store as it looked the morning we arrived in Atlin. Our sled," Mollie's shutter reveals a tent store with a large and well-painted sign, "General Merchandise." Hanging from and leaning against this temporary structure are hats, boots, boxes, shovels, doors and windows, axes and rope. Mollie and Tom's fully loaded sledge is parked in front. It was a long trip, and undoubtedly they were happy to have arrived. "I am the monarch of all I survey," a man — Tom? — standing atop a partially constructed log cabin, might make a pair with "Interior of our Atlin Cabin," two men reading in a cabin showing clothing hanging on hooks, boots, food and bottles on open shelves, fur rug, and rough bunks.

An Atlin winter scene.

A dangerous place
the Atlin trail.

Until fall 1898, the Brackett family in Skagway had remained one step removed from the actual mining of gold. Now they were to be actively involved in the highly speculative and practical work of seeking nuggets. It was a turning point, a new and less civilized life. "Atlin," wrote one of the writers of *The Skaguay News,* "has become the new miner's mecca."

On November 11, 1898 *The Skaguay News* carried an article entitled, "John Grant on Atlin." Mr. Grant, an "old Cassier war horse" had spent some time in Atlin and had

... no hesitation in saying that Atlin Lake [was] one of the finest placer mining sections ever opened in the province — perhaps not as rich as some parts of other famous camps, but with gold more generally diffused. In this estimate he does not except Cariboo or eastern Cassiar, the new diggings being in the western section of that great northern district. ... New prospects are being reported every day, with every chance of even greater ones being discovered. ... [T]here are sufficient claims in Atlin district to warrant employment, directly and indirectly, of 10,000 men, for the claims already taken up on all the creeks comes to 130 miles in total. ... Aside from mining possibilities Mr. Grant says ... the grass [is] so abundant that it is possible to graze many thousand head of cattle during the season. It offers capabilities, too, for dairying, and sufficient hay can be cut to support the animals throughout the snowy portion of the year. ... The road from ... Atlin City to discovery on Pine Creek, a distance of eight miles, could be made into a very good wagon road at small cost. ... Atlin City is quite a settle-

Another shadow "self-portrait" of the photographer can be seen in this late winter picture of eager gold-seekers digging under deep snow in Atlin.

BRATL037

94

BRATL035

Atlin, like Dawson City, was a Canadian town populated mostly by Americans.

A Winter camp.

A corduroy bridge
dog

ment already, and many houses have sprung up ... Most of the people there will spend the winter guarding their interests and getting ready for spring work. The climate is such an improvement over that of Lynn canal vicinity that hundreds of Indians go to Atlin every winter, saying it is much warmer and has an abundance of game. The summer climate is delightful.

For the optimistic newspaper writers of Skagway, every indication pointed toward rich rewards for gold prospectors in the Atlin gold fields. But Tom and Mollie needed a rest. As 1898 drew to a close, they traveled to Minneapolis for an extended visit probably leaving Al, Jim and Frank to represent the Brackett interests in Skagway and Atlin.

They returned on January 26, 1899 just in time to wave goodbye to Frank who, on a record for early outfitting over the pass, was demonstrating the "excellent condition of the trail between [Skagway] and Bennett." Packers were again cutting down toll gates on the Brackett wagon road. The couple must have felt they had arrived in the jaws of the sharks. There were always challenges in George Brackett's Alaska family enterprises. Mary probably settled in at Father Brackett's Skagway "mansion" while Tom worked as a packer.

Excitement was building as the winter waned. Track laying crews working for the new railroad had nearly reached the summit of White Pass, and a day-long celebration was planned. On Monday morning, February 20th, the stores were decorated and Skagway citizens paraded in the streets. The grand excursion was about to begin. "Mrs. Tom

"...a Merry Banquet in a Tent With the Thermometer Sulking on the Twenty-Second Step of the Cellar."

Brackett," Frank Brackett and Al Brackett had been invited as special guests. The February 21, 1899 *The Daily Alaskan* reported the event with tall headlines and much fanfare:

THE PROUDEST DAY IN ALSKA'S [sic] HISTORY

Celebration Under Two Flags, of Completion of
the Railroad to the Summit of White Pass

BLUE SKY — BRILLIANT SUNSHINE

Twenty Nine Hundred Feet Nearer to Heaven, the Eagle Cooed and the Lion Purred Together — a Merry Banquet in a Tent With the Thermometer Sulking on the Twenty-Second Step of the Cellar — Fair Women There to Inspire the Orators — A Second Banquet in Town to Commemorate the First.

Good Dame Nature, arrayed all in virgin white under a bright sun and a cloudless sky, smiled and looked her prettiest on the mighty bleak summit of the great White Pass yesterday, in honor of the arrival at that elevation of the first through passenger train ever sent out from Skaguay over the now famous White pass & Yukon Railroad. Everything combined to make the day a most enjoyable one [that will leave] a pleasant recollection in the minds of the one hundred guests who were invited to witness the completion of the gigantic undertaking of building a railroad to the summit, to the end of the American line and the commencement of the same line on British Columbia territory on toward Bennett. ...

It was four degrees below zero at the start with an unpleasant cold north wind ... and as the train whirled along the side of the mountain and gained elevation it grew cold, until at the summit the mercury dropped to 22

BRSGY091

"Sharp-shooters" Railroad excursion Feb. 30th 1899

657.

"WHITE PASS AND YUKON ROUTE"

FIRST PASSENGER TRAIN ON THE SUMMIT OF WHITE PASS. FEB. 20- 1899.

By the time Mr. Hegg took this photo Mollie had already put away her camera. She can be seen standing in the second row, perched on the locomotive, second person on our right from the man wearing the striped coat.

degrees below. The cars, however, were comfortably heated and the fur coats, parkies [sic] and other Arctic wearing apparel worn by a large number of guests were only comfortable on the summit and out in the bracing air of that elevation. Traffic manager Gray ... overlooked nothing, not even a photographer, and Mr. Hegg made it his business to take a number of views of the train and its passengers. ... Beside Mr. Hegg there were [K]odaks and cameras enough on board to have made a good start for a camera club. These were ... Mrs. Thomas Brackett, Messrs ... Frank Brackett ... [etc]. All these lined up at every stop and formed an interesting, picturesque group of themselves which it is hoped was secured by Mr. Hegg.

... The first glimpse of the summit was the sight of two flag poles within about 50 feet of each other, the one flying the stars and stripes, the other the Union Jack ...

"'Sharp-shooters.' Railroad excursion Feb. 20th, 1899," Mollie's record of the excursion shows just what *The Daily Alaskan* reporter suggested Hegg's photo might show — a picturesque group of photographers snapping the occasion. Two of Mr. Hegg's glass plate negatives survive, although Mollie Brackett's snapshot apparently was made at a different stop.

By the end of April, 1899 all the trails were impassable with melting snow, the thawing lakes dangerous, and May Day offered the excuse for a party. *The Daily Alaskan* advertised:

MAY POLE DANCE TOMORROW NIGHT
 by the Ladies of the Presbyterian Church
 Handsome May Queen and Her Suite Will Make Her

> **"The young Bracketts were well known in the Skagway community, and Mollie could be counted on to entertain by singing and playing the piano."**

Entrance at 8 O'clock - Five Booths Where Money Can Handily be Spent and Good Returns Given.

Everyone is looking forward to the pleasure of the May Day Festival ... the Ladies one and all, married and in the state of single blessedness, have been untiring in their efforts to make it a pronounced success.

...A musical programme has been arranged for each evening, in which Mrs. Tom Brackett, Mrs. T. Whitten, Mr. Holmquist and Mr. Diffin will take part.

The young Bracketts were well known in the Skagway community, and Mollie could be counted on to entertain by singing and playing the piano.

Now that George had less construction and fund raising to occupy his time, he entertained friends and relatives, particularly in the mild Alaska summers. For "An 'Early June' Picnic," Mollie snapped a large group of her relatives, including brother-in-law Al, Ida and their four children, George, Percy, Bertha and Kathryn; Karl, youngest of the seven Brackett brothers; George Augustus Brackett and a number of family friends.

According to *The Skagway News,* on Tuesday, June 27, 1899 Skagway honored Senator Fairbanks and a distinguished party of officers and women.

The entire party, including the officers of the boat met the reception committee of the Chamber of Commerce at Moore's wharf and the ladies were driven to the residence of Geo. A. Brackett. The gentlemen of the party spent the forenoon in a walk through the city. ... In the afternoon an informal musical was given in No. 2's hall at which most of the senatorial party was present. Mrs.

BRSGY080

Al. Brackett. Percy   G. Brackett Jr. Mr. Jennings Karl Brackett.

Cordelia Dams. Baby Jennings.   Mrs Pugh.   Mrs. Holmquist.

Mrs Jennings.   Bertha Zela Brackett.

An "Early June" Picnic.   Katherine.   G. A. B.

The "General" with Governor Brady's Children. August '95

BRSGY096

Thomas Brackett and Mr. Holmquist, with Mrs. A. L. Cheney at the piano, entertained ... with a number of vocal selections concluding with a beautiful duet. The affair was charmingly informal, and at its conclusion the party, accompanied by the reception committee and members of the press, enjoyed a short ride up the wagon road.

The members of Senator Fairbanks' party were highly entertained at an impromptu gathering at the home of Mr. Brackett on Wednesday evening after their conference with the Chamber of Commerce. Vocal and instrumental music, with a rubber of whist, served as a welcome change to the worthy guests, allowing them a much needed rest while passing a charming hour. Those present were the members of the senatorial party, Capt. Coulson and Dr. Carpenter of the McCulloch, Gov. Brady, Mr. and Mrs. Cheney, ... Mr. and Mrs. Alfred Brackett, Mr. and Mrs. Thomas Brackett ...

Mollie, Tom, Ida and Al teamed with George to entertain important visitors to Alaska. A widower, George Brackett came to depend on his daughters-in-law to provide social niceties for his guests.

But rounds of active social life soon were to give way to hard work and adventure as the Brackett family became enmeshed in the new wave of gold fever sweeping Skagway. *The Daily Alaskan* 1900 New Year's Edition carried a feature story that could almost have been written by Mollie herself.

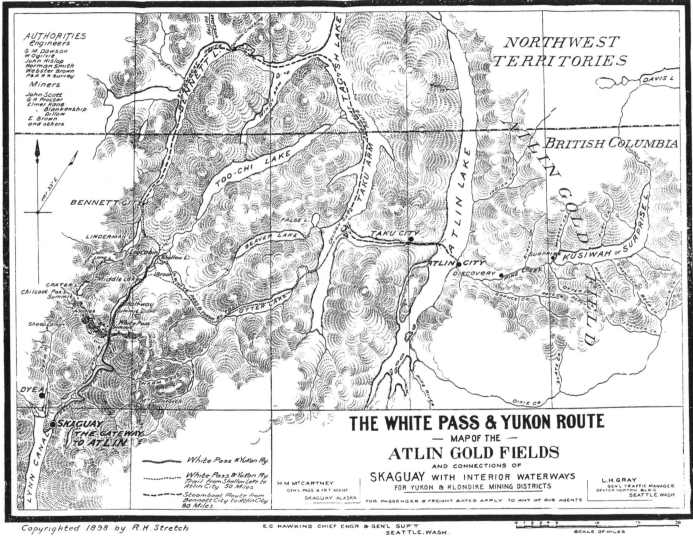

AUTHORITIES
Engineers
G. M. Dawson
W Ogilvie
John Hislop
Norman Smith
Webster Brown
P & A R R survey
Miners.
John Scott
G R Procter
Elmer Kane
Blankenship
Dillow
E. Brown
and others

NORTHWEST
TERRITORIES

DAVIS L

BRITISH COLUMBIA

ATLIN GOLD FIELD

BENNETT L.

TAG-ISH LAKE

TOO-CHI LAKE

BENNETT CITY

LINDERMAN

FALSE L.

BEAVER LAKE

TAKU CITY

ATLIN LAKE

KUSIWAH or SURPRISE L.

SURPRISE

Log Cabin

Shallow L.

Brooks

Middle Lake

ATLIN CITY

DISCOVERY

PINE CREEK

OTTER LAKE

CRATER

Chilcoot Pass
Summit

Scales

Halfway

Sheep Camp

White Pass
Summit

DYEA

SPRUCE CR

SLATE CR

PIKE RIVER

DIXIE CR

SKAGUAY
THE GATEWAY
TO ATLIN

LYNN CANAL

Mt Carystich

White Pass & Yukon Ry.

White Pass & Yukon Ry.
Trail from Shallow Lake to
Atlin City   50 Miles

Steamboat Route from
Bennett City to Atlin City
80 Miles

THE WHITE PASS & YUKON ROUTE
— MAP OF THE —
ATLIN GOLD FIELDS
AND CONNECTIONS OF
SKAGUAY WITH INTERIOR WATERWAYS
FOR YUKON & KLONDIKE MINING DISTRICTS

FOR PASSENGER & FREIGHT RATES APPLY TO ANY OF OUR AGENTS

H. M. M^cCARTNEY
GEN'L PASS & FR'T AGENT
SKAGUAY ALASKA

L. H. GRAY
GEN'L TRAFFIC MANAGER
DEXTER HORTON BLD'G
SEATTLE, WASH.

Copyrighted 1898 by R. H. Stretch

E. C. HAWKINS CHIEF ENG'R & GEN'L SUP'T
SEATTLE, WASH.

SCALE OF MILES

Summer in Atlin's Mining Camps

Mollie Brackett was not the only woman to experience the miners' life in Atlin. If Mollie had left us her journal or some letters they might have described adventures very similar to those remembered in this account by Nellie Runnals.

"... the railroad to the summit has robbed that difficult climb of its terrors ..."

From The Daily Alaskan, New Year's Edition 1900

SUMMER IN ATLIN'S MINING CAMPS
By Mrs. H. B. Runnalls

Since the railroad to the summit has robbed that difficult climb of its terrors, and made the long tedious journey from Skagway to Bennett a rather tame affair of a few hours, one has only memory of olfactory discomfort from the crowds which pressed too near, and the unfading picture of sublimity which impressed itself upon our retina from the awful and everlasting hills, as souvenirs of the summer morning upon which we began the trip to meet my husband in Atlin. There I was to pass some time in a famous mining camp in which was centered the hopes and expectations of a multitude of eager anxious men, and women, too, who for the most part had made sacrifices, sometimes incredible, to join the ranks of sanguine seekers after the yellow metal, supposed to be waiting only a strong arm to yield itself up to the uses and necessities of man. Alas! alack aday! how crestfallen and crushed were many of them as they turned away to other fields, always just a little further on, having seen their hopes of success in Atlin become forlorn. But let me not anticipate.

Summit gained, we learned that dynamite had been

"The water had flooded us to the knees and constant bailing out with five gallon cans by burly men had threatened to be inadequate ..."

used to tear away a passage for a tiny boat through the ice on the lake which covers the basin on top of the mountain, and with trepidation at the sight of the crowd in such a frail craft we ventured to board her, and lived to see the other shore gained, after experiencing great fear and trembling and wet skirts and general misery and hope deferred; for [when] the bow was under the ice and again we slid upon a block and our strong pilot, who with a pole pushed aside the great iceberg, and guided his barge as best he could, was almost helpless to accomplish his task, which finished perhaps in spite of him. The water had flooded us to the knees and constant bailing out with five gallon cans by burly men had threatened to be inadequate to the dire situation. But, as sunshine after a storm brings cheer and relief, at last the weary miles of icy way was made to the finish, and none too soon, for many were so chilled that it is a marvel if some not so robust as myself do not reap a bundle of rheumatic pains in the years to come, as the harvest of that day's sowing.

We jolted in wagons down to Log Cabin through streets of tents. It was the very first log house that gave a name to the busy town which afterwards grew around the northwest mounted police headquarters. And it was a perfectly frantic and eager crowd which pushed and jostled trying to hurry the officials about the business of clearing their numerous effects. Only the wise man who had traveled and knows the "open sesame" was the one able to make time in that operation. Finally, however, we continued on our way, still in wagons, to Bennett. May I dare to say what a sad impression was made upon my mind by the

> *"... I saw a grave marked by a wooden cross ... the resting place of a man ... crushed by the loss of his outfit ..."*

sight of this naked village, set upon the edge of the barren rock, which seems the very end of the world, so forbidding and iron-bound in its prison-like aspect. As I saw a grave marked by a wooden cross, which I was told was the resting place of a man who had, "cut the cord" of life perfectly crushed by the loss of his outfit, I wondered that he had no companions in his solitary last home. And even I could have calmly laid me down to sleep also crushed by the overhanging grimness of all nature about me: 12 o'clock p. m., hotels all full, sitting perched up in a wagon whilst the driver was vainly hunting a bunk, cold and miserable, feeling friendless and alone. But one does not always die because nature is unsympathetic, and, indeed, if we only read her meaning aright, her very changeableness ought to keep us assured of the good faith and fidelity of a higher supreme power, always steadfast however life cheats us.

The next morning the sun shone at Bennett upon the just and the unjust as elsewhere, and having spent a fairly comfortable night, I took courage to live and walk aboard the steamer *Gleaner* which was to carry us between the lowering mountains that line each side of the arm and reach around to Taku. After a few miles the lake widens out, the rocky barriers slope back and green beaches break the horror of bare rocks; verdant isles dot the waters while the shadows lengthen, and opal hues delight the eyes. Softened nature moves me to a more cheerful mood. Long day, unending twilight and sunrise meeting, the soft gentle adieu of the light which so soon faded as softly reappears, all fill the mind with such wonder at the miracle enacting that we land at the portage at four o'clock a. m. as in a dream. I had not been asleep once during the night, my mind so completely taken up with the constantly changing panorama.

I walk the two and one-half miles through green woods of quivering aspen with carpet of heavenly green, the dye of a million spikes of flowers lavishes itself upon the grateful senses, the birds sing and a fleecy cloudy sky beams upon us — this is my introduction to the real Atlin country. While summer lasts, it is a paradise, if one is only poet and dreamer and can live upon nature prestine [sic]. In time this earth may yield to science treasures of commerce other than mineral, but today one's dinner must come out of a tin can, for man is too busy looking for nuggets to trouble about tilling the soil. Later on, however, I noticed patches of growing oats and other grains, self sown where the horses had fed on their way, proving that the climate will permit of the cultivation of cereals. Native berries to the number of eleven varieties, which during the season I saw growing in greater or lesser abundance, go to promise a living to the brave pioneer who will settle this north land in the future, and wrest from it his fare in the good old way of our first parent.

A short trip of eight miles from the Taku portage, by a very decent little steamer, the Scotia, took us to the famous city of Atlin. And truly, if first impressions go for anything, one ought to feel paid for coming, since it would be hard to find a site more admirable, a view more enchanting than that which gladdens the vision as one steams down this most beautiful sheet of water. The several islands lying

"... the large buildings are softened by dark towering hemlock and spruce and the delicate shining of the poplar."

opposite show shelving beaches, green spires of pine, and long shadows that fill the glacial waters with rich color. The white tents and trim cabins, the more pretentious looking buildings, stores, banks, hotels, etc., cover the sloping height, the clean streets are bordered with grass and the outlines of the large buildings are softened by dark towering hemlock and spruce and the delicate shimmering of the poplar. All this quiet beauty under fleecy clouds in the blue sky of a June day; and you may imagine if the wife brought a bright face to the waiting husband. We had short looks for the neat stores and shops, or the by this time familiar mining man who had on my first advent to this northern land awakened so much interest by his appearance, so unconventional and often outlandish.

I leave the town without regret, however, and wend my way in a spring wagon eight miles to Discovery, my destination. What a charming drive through pine groves, beside murmuring streams, in sight of grand vistas and delightful hillsides and valleys past road house and lunch stand making a welcome in harmony sometimes, with the awe inspiring surroundings. Roads good, frequent meetings of one's kind and general air of business, almost give the lie to the perfect infancy of this civilization.

At Nugget Point, ten minutes' walk from the town of Discovery, I was made acquainted with my tent home, which under two white roofs was to make my habitation for three months. If one has seen a man's housekeeping, words of mine are unnecessary to explain the scene on which my eyes rested when first I looked upon my husband's household goods; but taking my courage in my

109

"... there was always the
hope and expectation of
finding the big nuggets ..."

teeth, applying wit and woman's skill joined to some yards of cheap drapery and a few skins of beasts, the result was quite astonishing and luxurious, and our home became the rendezvous for all the homeless men of our acquaintance. As is common in all mining camps, these men reverenced a little woman who in a small way did what she could to make up to her friends for all they missed in that new country, so far from their hearts' homes.

Soon mining was the absorbing topic. I learned to pan and became quite an adept in finding pay gravel, and to understand the jargon and vernacular of the camp. Sluicing and rocking was only the sequel to a great deal of hard work and expenditure of money, and the net result was not always wildly exciting. But there was always the hope and expectation of finding the big nuggets, and although you might get off the pay streak for a while it was sure to crop out again by following it up. Many were disappointed, however, what with spring floods and unevenness of the deposit, and came out very far from even. Atlin, it is thought, will pay the capitalist who can bring hydraulics to bear upon vast acres of alluvial soil, and large companies are now organized to buy up and work the whole country. I am still holding some bench claims which I hope to sell. I had the pleasure of locating and staking them myself. Once I went on a prospecting trip but did not stake. One never to be forgotten day a much beguiled friend came at dawn to announce a "quiet tip," a creek full of prospects just over the hills a bit, and a day would do to investigate it. With what spirit and expectation we trudged away through bush and marsh, up hill and down dale, exasperated by the

*"... I have lots of nuggets
that I myself washed,
and bounding health
and spirits ..."*

mosquitoes, hour after hour till, fainting and almost exhausted, at 2 p. m. we arrived at the Eldorado of our dream almost dead beat by our eighteen-mile walk. My husband and the other men dug graves for our hopes, for they found not a color; and when by the sweat of his brow he was earning experience, the trumpet of the heavens sounded the warning and down poured the vials of wrath upon our Sunday desecration. We crept under the bushes but were drenched in three seconds by buckets of the wettest of rain, and only a gold pan stood between my face and the unmerciful washing I was being treated to. Indeed, the test was too severe, for upon creeping into a friendly tent a few miles on, I gave out and laid myself down sans coleur, sans esprit, and completely collapsed for the nonce. But with coffee and bread and much praise for my bravery, my courage came to the front and somehow home was won after all. And Bed, oh! bliss! Two whole days it claimed me.

But I have lots of nuggets that I myself washed, and bounding health and spirits, and the reward of whatever hardship I experienced in my summer's outing. I visited every creek in the district, sometimes riding but more often walking, as the horses were very poor and no livery keeper cared to rent me a horse more than once, as they required too long a rest afterwards. I went hunting for duck and ptarmigan, and found them too; and I killed grayling and trout in Pine creek, which is in itself a host of fun. The grayling is a gamey fellow not easy to land, but toothsome and fit for a king when cooked with bacon. I sketched, painted, twanged guitar and, in general, ate lotus flowers of ease and enjoyment. On cold or rainy days I would develop films and print pictures, for in all my wanderings I was never without my Eastman. I had, too, my favorite books with me, so was never lonely.

I gathered over forty varieties of wild flowers, notable among which were the wild roses, violets, lupins [sic], forget-me-nots, azaleas, iris, columbines and even orchids. The summer, indeed, was one long picnic, every day too short and each one full of the delight of life. We had many delightful afternoon teas in our tent and on the claims, and some exciting rubbers of whist in the evening.

Sundays I religiously attended the Episcopal church, often being the only lady present. Although there was no organ, never have I heard the hymns and canticles sung better than by these earnest, thoughtful, sturdy miners that comprised the congregation.

I left Atlin October 13th for Skagway, feeling that the summer just past had been one of the pleasantest of my life, and am now wintering on a rocky hillside in a log cabin, trying to cultivate my mind and patience as I wait for another springtime to experience anew the delights of an Alaska mining camp.

— *Nellie C. Runnalls*

The Bracketts in Atlin

Building a head dam

On the way to Surprise Lake G. A. B. Gold Commissioner Graham.

By summer 1899 Atlin and gold had become the new focus of most of the Bracketts. In Mollie's "Nugget point, Pine Creek, Caledonian Group" the hodge podge of scattered tents on both sides of the 30-foot creek is laced with cribs and sluiceways directing water for various gold ventures. The ripped and shoveled land in what may once have been a lovely pasture has been reduced to chaos. The rush of men and equipment over the 85-mile trail to support a venture the size of the Atlin gold rush took a host of "Packers, cooks and caches." Mollie photographed this motley group of dogs and men resting before another frantic plunge over the wilderness track. In "Father Panning Gold," a posed shot, George, attired in hat and three-piece suit adorned with watch fob, sits, high rubber booted feet in stream. Behind him are some of the giant sluiceways built to catch tons of earth forced from the hillsides by water pressure from huge hoses. Hydraulic mining was the order of the day in Atlin, and Brackett was promoting this new venture with a folksy photo for his investors. "Building a head dam" is a more forthright picture of what was actually happening.

"A dinner party at Camp Discovery, Aug. 1899," Frank, George, Mollie, Karl and perhaps Gold Commissioner Graham outside a log cabin, may have been taken by Tom. "On the way to Surprise Lake, G. A. B., Gold Commissioner Graham" is a telling shot of George showing the commissioner the territory and perhaps his claims. An untiring promoter and entertainer of dignitaries, Mollie's father-in-law often enlisted her help in hosting politicians, his friends, acquaintances and group excursions. And she

113

Nuggut Point. Pine Creek.   Caledonian Group

BRATL017

Hydraulic mining was practical along the creeks around Atlin because water was plentiful and the topography permitted it to flow with gravity. Large log and stonework dams and a network of wooden flumes were constructed to contain the water and direct it through sluices to wash out gold. (NOTE: Recent evidence indicates that the dam shown on page 115, thought to have been built near Atlin, was actually located at Dewey Lakes Reservoir above Skagway).

BRATL019

Father Panning gold.

BRATL018

A dinner party at Camp above Discovery, Aug. 1899.

The quality of paydirt is assessed at one of the Brackett claims by blowing away sand taken from sample pans to separate the gold by gravity. Notice the balance scale on the table between the two men. In photo on page 119, Jim (right) and friends take time out from working a Klondike claim.

JAMES BRACKETT   N₀ 2 ADAMS GULCH

BRATL012

Packers, Cooks and cache.

BRATL031

Tommie and his Arabian Steed

*George A. Brackett had a keen instinct
for cultivating people who could be
helpful to his enterprises. William B. Close
was one of the major financial backers of
the White Pass & Yukon Route railroad.

probably cooked for this crew. She stands in the background, hand on hip, perhaps amused by the men's poses.

In a letter to G.A.B. from W. B. Close,* Chicago, written on Sept. 9th, 1899, Close thanks the family thus:

"I must first take this opportunity of thanking you, Mr. & Mrs. Tom Bracket [sic] and your family generally for the great kindness and courtesy you showed our party. We only hope that we may have the opportunity some day of reciprocating. ..."

With day-to-day mining operations in the hands of his sons, the patriarch now spent significant time promoting Alaska, working politically to define the boundary between Canada and the United States, and entertaining congressmen and their families. His daughter-in-law Mollie may have stood in as his social director.

The "boys" were also hard at work. "Tommie and his Arabian Steed" were packing, sometimes overturning in difficult locations as we see in "The 'turn over.' Caribou Crossing."

When in Skagway, the Bracketts' lives were rather civilized. Newspaper ads such as, "Have you seen the handsome bathtub and fixtures at Brownell's," "Fine toilet seats cannot be equalled outside Baker's" and "Keep your house warm by banking up the outside with sand or manure." "We deliver the material - Alaska Transfer Co." peppered the pages of the two local newspapers.

On December 17, 1899 *The Daily Alaskan* recorded:

The dancing party given by the social club ... was well attended and thoroughly enjoyed by the society folk of Skaguay at Fireman's Hall Monday night.

The "turn over". Carcton Crossing

Arrangement of the dances was highly satisfactory: the music furnished by E. H. Martinson's famous orchestra, was splendid, and the fair of Skaguay, in its charming attire, was superb, so there is not a wonder that all are highly enthusiastic over the delightful affair.

Among the "Mesdames" and "Messrs" present were the Bracketts, probably fresh off the trail.

Mollie's less frivolous father-in-law spent part of the Christmas holidays dispensing wisdom. At a Skagway Chamber of Commerce dinner on December 22, 1899, *The Daily Alaskan* reported, *"George A. Brackett wagged that long beard ... to the tune of much real wisdom on the question of schools. Mr. Brackett said that all we had to do was to ask for a $5000 or two $5000 buildings for school purposes, and get it, and the Chamber appointed a committee right off to do the asking."* George was utilizing his experience as former mayor of Minneapolis to impress Skagway businessmen.

On Sunday, January 7, 1900 *The Daily Alaskan* reported, *"Miss Gould, who has been the guest of Mr. and Mrs. A. H. Brackett the last several weeks, left during the week for her home in Minneapolis ... Mr. George A. Brackett left Thursday for the east where he will spend the winter. He will return to Skaguay in April."* It is probable that Frank and Jim may have been supervising the Atlin claims while Al tended to his father's business in Skagway.

Spring brought copper discoveries near Whitehorse, the usual calamities of teams falling through ice on the lakes at break up, and more and more residents of the lower states coming to Alaska on excursions to view the

123

"The Bracketts ... have found the earth rich ..."

outback as a curiosity. The White Pass & Yukon Railway promoted itself as the "Scenic Route of the World." According to local newspaper accounts, "The Pacific Coast Steamship Company put three steamers in the Alaskan excursion trade," and *"Nearly a hundred of the prettiest of pretty girls and handsome women, dressed in the most artistic and fantastic styles, with shimmering satin banners of all hues of the rainbow, made a kaleidoscope of such brilliantly beautiful coloring as has never been seen before in Skaguay."*

On May 5th, *"The little misses Catherine and Bertha Brackett entertained a number of their little friends at their home in the afternoon."* On May 8th *"James Brackett and bride arrived ... on the Rosalie. Mrs. Brackett was Miss Mamie Gould. The happy couple were married in Minneapolis lately, and started for Skaguay immediately afterward. Mrs. Brackett visited Skaguay last winter and is well known here. Mr. Brackett is the son of George A. Brackett and is a pioneer of Skaguay."*

Throughout 1900 the papers speculate on Brackett claims at Atlin. Under the May 11th headline "SLUICING HAS BEGUN ON ATLIN'S CREEKS" in *The Daily Alaskan*, was the following:

This season's output is over $5,000,000 on Brackett claims. ... The Bracketts are going to run a big flume over their property along bedrock, and have found the earth rich right where they have dug the trench for the flume. They have taken out a bottle full of the yellow metal. More gold will be taken out of this Brackett property on Willow this season than was taken from the entire district

> *"There is no Alaskan prouder of his sons than Mr. Brackett, and there is probably no man who has the right to be so proud ..."*

of Atlin last year. Eighty men are at work on the property making preparation for the season's operations.

When George Brackett arrived in Skagway from Atlin on June 7th he stated, "I have nothing extravagant to report in regard to Atlin. Atlin has yet to be proved ..." Then on July 8th *The Daily Alaskan* again confirmed, *"... the Bracketts have been taking out large quantities of gold for some time. ... They [have] on hand about 400 pounds of the precious metal, approaching $80,000 in value."* And when Brackett again arrived in town September 19th, he offered, "We have taken out enough, perhaps, to pay expenses. But we have property there on Willow Creek that it will take us five years to work out, and our stockholders must be satisfied with the result. Further than that I am not at liberty to tell you."

On October 11, 1900 *The Daily Alaskan* reported:

George Brackett came in on the evening train yesterday, with Jim Brackett and his wife, and Tom Brackett all by himself and Al Brackett was at the depot to give them welcome. There is no Alaskan prouder of his sons than Mr. Brackett, and there is probably no man who has the right to be so proud of his sons. ...

"Mr. Thomas Brackett ... will leave shortly for Boston," reported the October 14, 1900 *The Daily Alaskan*. But in all of 1900 in the Skagway newspapers there is no mention of his wife Mollie.

In 1890 the population of Alaska was 32,052. By 1900 it had almost doubled to 63,441, but Mollie apparently was no longer there among the pioneers. Her months in Alaska had been a good time for Mary Montgomery Brackett.

Afterword

O n February 26, 1901 in the Portsmouth, New Hampshire home of his wife's mother, Thomas Thayer Brackett died of typhoid fever, his wife and father by his bedside. Tom's obituary states:

"... He was twenty-eight years old. Mr. Brackett married Miss Mary Montgomery of Portsmouth. Mrs. Brackett immediately won a high place for herself among musicians in Minneapolis and was for some time soprano at Westminster Church. ..."

At Tom's funeral on March 1, 1901, in his closing words, the minister spoke to God of Mollie saying,

"Thou hast come early in the joy of her wedded life and thus given her this burden to bear and bear always. The one whom she loved and whom she honored and to whom she has given body and heart, has been stricken down by this disease and today we carry away all that is left of him; the spirit has passed on to God that gave it. Father! Come to her heart in grief. May she not turn away from God but to God in her great sorrow."

"Dear Old Tom"
Just as he was.
August
1898.

BRWHP184

After the funeral, Mollie wrote a caption to a fine snapshot of Tom: "'Dear Old Tom' just as he *was*. August 1898." He stands dressed for an excursion with his bow tie slightly askew, looking at the photographer, the mountains towering over the Skagway River valley in the distance.

In 1910 at a testimonial dinner for George A. Brackett by the Publicity Club of Minneapolis on Wednesday evening April 13,

"Mrs. Thomas Thayer Brackett, daughter-in-law of the guest of honor, well-known in Minneapolis as a vocalist, and now singing in one of New York's leading churches, was graciously introduced by the toastmaster and sang, 'Ben Bolt,' and a group of other ballads which evoked tremendous applause."

News of the death of Mary Emmeline Montgomery Brackett was reported in Portsmouth on July 22, 1939 by *The New Hampshire Weekly Gazette:*

"... She had a beautiful soprano voice and was prominent in musical circles, and had many friends. For a number of years she was a member of the quartette of the Middle Street Baptist Church and teacher of voice.

"Mrs. Brackett had made her home in California for a number of years where she was also active in musical circles in La Jolla. ... She had a delightful personality and news of her death is heard with much regret by her friends here."

Mary Brackett Ballard, 88 years old in 1996, has not forgotten her aunt: *"She really mourned her husband. I can remember Aunt Mollie urged my mother, also a Brackett brother widow, to come visit her in La Jolla, but she was not so adventurous."*

And later, *"The only other thing I remember about my Aunt Mollie is a song she taught me when I was seven or eight:*

> *Sweetest little fella,*
> *Everybody knows.*
> *Don't know what to call him,*
> *but he's mighty like a rose!*
> *Looking at his mommy*
> *with eyes so shiny blue.*
> *Makes you think that heaven*
> *is comin' close to you."*

Thank you, great-aunt Mary Montgomery Brackett and great-grandfather George Augustus Brackett for your stories.

—Cynthia Brackett Driscoll, January 1996